Tonka®

IF I COULD DRIVE A TANKER TRUCK!

by Michael Teitelbaum
Pencils by Richard Courtney
Color by Marc Mones

SCHOLASTIC INC.
New York Toronto London Auckland Sydney
Mexico City New Delhi Hong Kong Buenos Aires

Special thanks to Denny Brockway and George Key of Hobart, NY, for all their help.
—Michael Teitelbaum

Many thanks to the Terry Winder Family and Mickey Durbin of the Dairy Farmers of America for their help in the production of this book. They represent all those who suffered loss of life and property in the tornado outbreak of May 4, 2003.
—Richard Courtney

Published by Scholastic Inc.
SCHOLASTIC and associated logos are trademarks and/or registered trademarks of Scholastic Inc.

Library of Congress Cataloging-in-Publication Data Available

ISBN 0-439-54835-7

10 9 8 7 6 5 4 3 2 04 05 06 07

Printed in the U.S.A.
First printing, March 2004

My name is George. My favorite toy is my new tanker truck! I love pushing it over to the farm to pick up milk.

After my tanker truck is filled, I pretend to drive it a long way to deliver fresh milk to lots of people.

What if I could drive a tanker truck?

I would drive from dairy farm to dairy farm, filling up my tanker truck with milk.

Tonka

My tanker truck is made up of two parts.

The first part is called the tractor. The tractor holds the cab. That's where I sit when I drive.

The other part of my tanker truck is called the trailer. The big tank that holds the milk is part of the trailer. An electric pump moves the milk in and out of the tank.

Farmers milk their cows every day. They store the milk in big containers called *bulk tanks*. Bulk tanks are refrigerated to keep the milk cold.

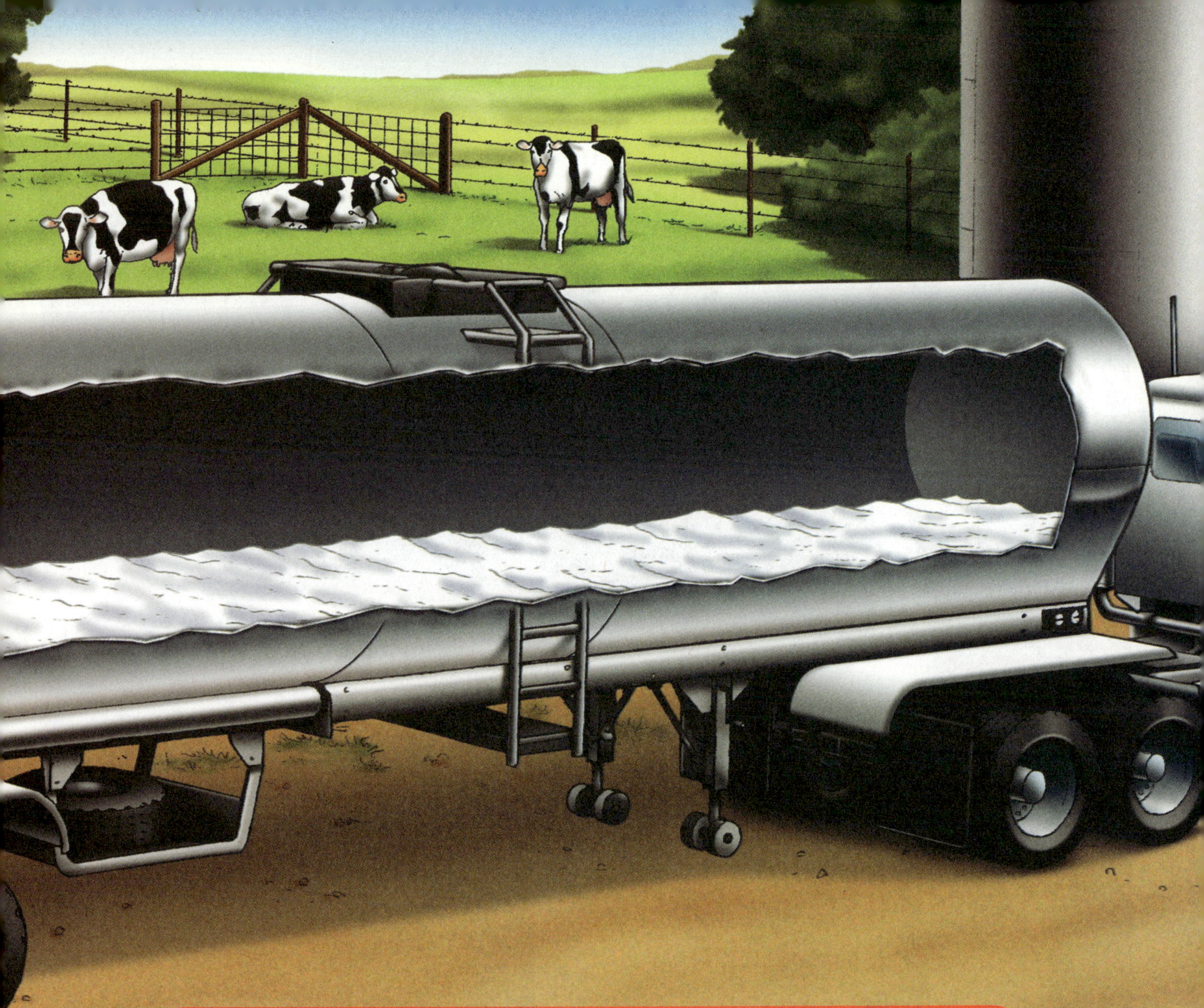

After I show up, I plug in my electric pump. Then the milk is pumped from the bulk tank into my tanker.

The inside of my tank is lined with glass, just like a thermos bottle. The milk inside can stay cold for two full days — even in the summertime!

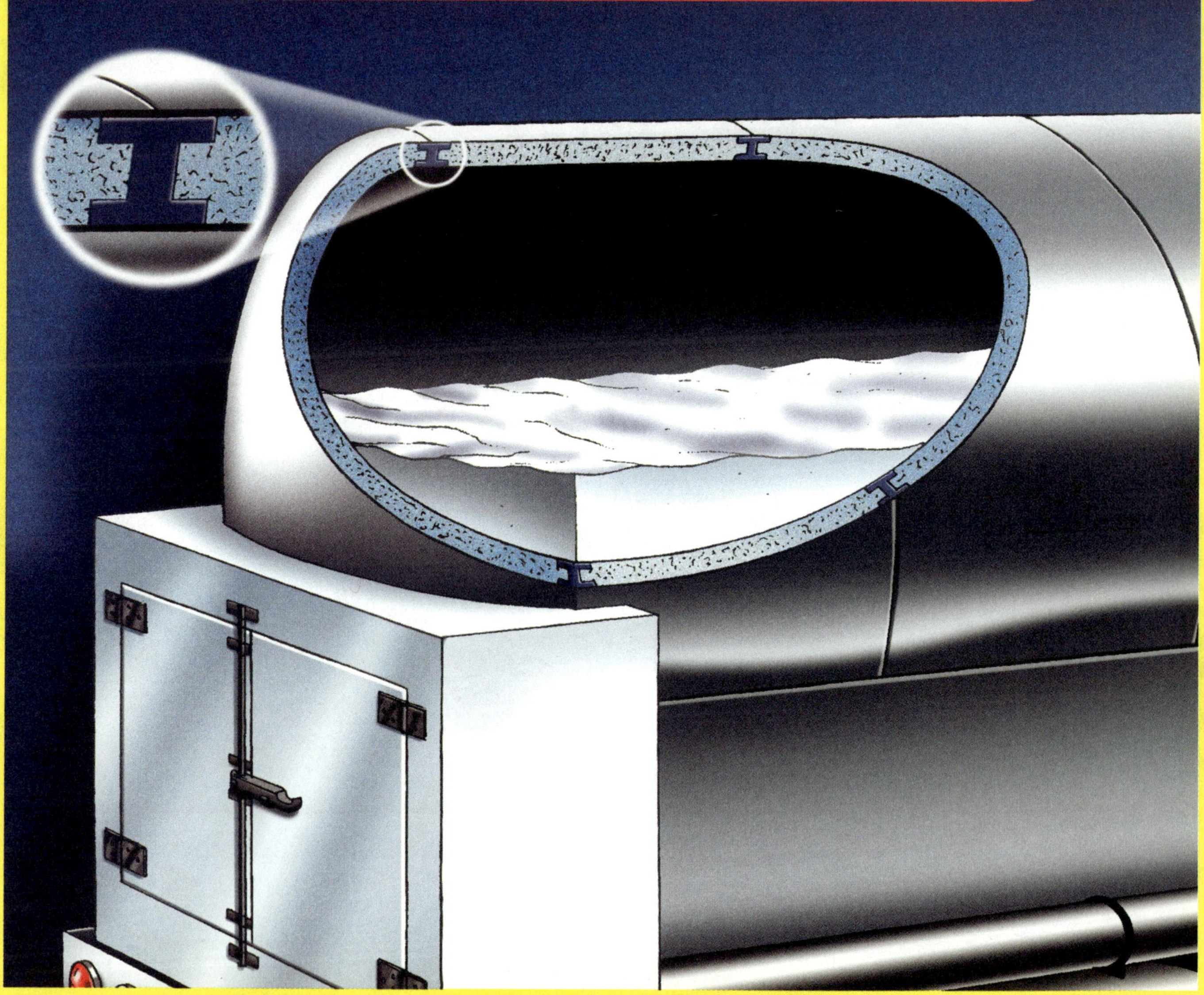

My truck's tank holds 7,000 gallons of milk. I have to stop at seven or eight farms to fill it all the way up.
Tonka

When my tank is full, I drive a long distance to bring the milk to a dairy. Sometimes I drive more than 400 miles in one day!

My tanker truck is safer to drive when it's completely full. That way the milk doesn't slosh around and shake the truck.

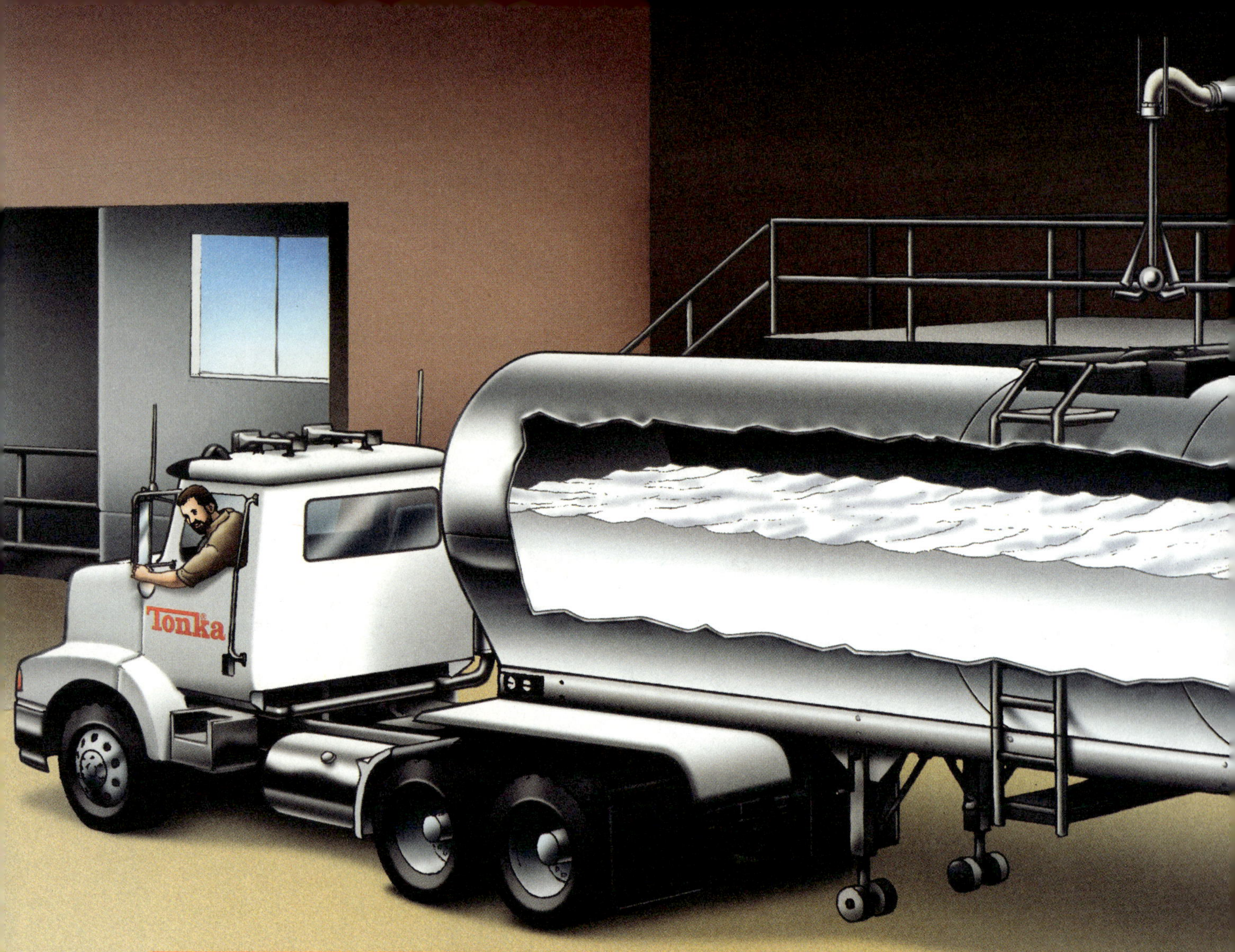

When I get to the dairy, I pump the milk from my tank into a giant milk silo. It takes eight or nine deliveries to fill the silo.

Then the milk is treated and poured into cartons or bottles. After that, it's shipped to stores so everybody can enjoy fresh milk.

Tonka®

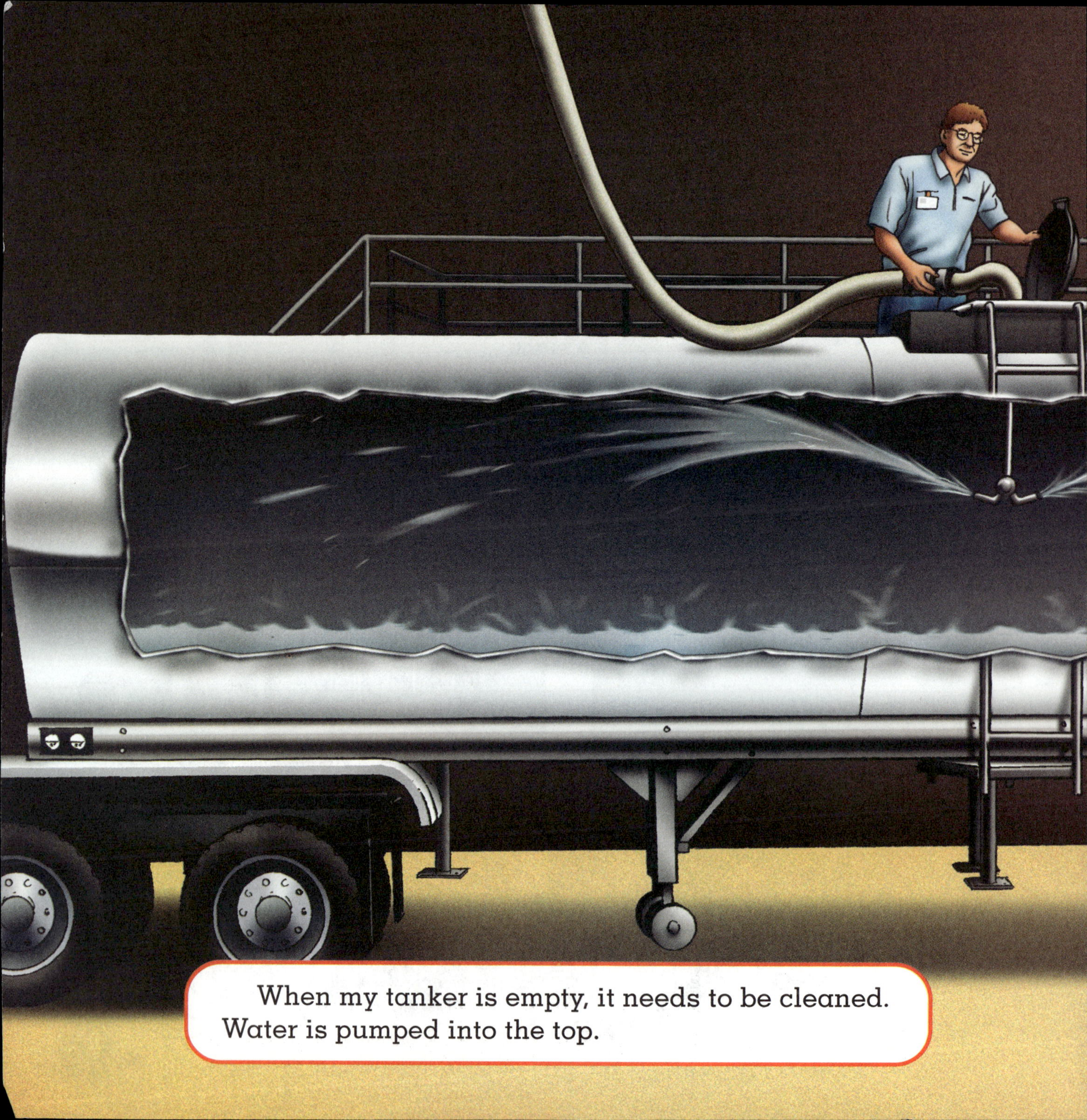

When my tanker is empty, it needs to be cleaned. Water is pumped into the top.

Then the water is pumped out the back.
Now I'm ready to pick up more milk!

Sometimes old milk tanker trucks are bought by fire departments. The firefighters use them to carry water to fires where there are no hydrants.

Today I am driving a different tanker truck. It delivers fuel oil to people's homes. The fuel oil heats their houses. I pump the oil into a large underground storage tank.

My fuel tanker truck also brings gasoline to gas stations. I deliver the gasoline into a huge underground tank beneath the pumps. Now it's ready to fill up cars.

This tanker truck delivers fuel to planes at the airport. An airplane is too big to fill up at a gas station!

I'd deliver lots of different kinds of liquids if I could drive a tanker truck!